Praise for TKO Series

"Dave Anderson's TKO series is a genuine knockout! The fast flowing format combined with high-impact content ensures that readers in any business and in any country will benefit from the universally sound principles presented."

—Sir Peter Vardy, former chairman and CEO of Reg Vardy PLC

"Leadership guru Dave Anderson's new TKO series guides you through the most important management moments in an innovative, down-to-earth, and short format. These highly readable, action-packed guides bring Anderson's insights straight into your world, usable from the CEO to the newest trainee."

—James Strock, author, *Theodore Roosevelt on Leadership*

"Want to go the distance and be a champion? Let Dave Anderson add power to your punch. The TKO series is loaded with hard-hitting strategies that will knock your competition out of contention."

—Randy Pennington, author, *Results Rule!: Build a Culture that Blows the Competition Away!*

"Don't be fooled by the slim size of Dave Anderson's TKO series books—they each pack a knockout punch. Forget sales and management theory, these bantamweight books hit right at the gut of your business—what you must to do succeed. Quick reads—and if applied, they'll provide you with life-long results."

—Paul McCord, author, *How to Build a Million Dollar Sales Income through Referrals*

TKO HIRING!

TKO HIRING!

TEN KNOCKOUT STRATEGIES *for* *Recruiting, Interviewing,* and *Hiring Great People*

DAVE ANDERSON

John Wiley & Sons, Inc.

Published by John Wiley & Sons, Inc., Hoboken, New Jersey.
Published simultaneously in Canada.

For general information on our other products and services or for technical support, please contact our Customer Care Department within the United States at (800) 762-2974, outside the United States at (317) 572-3993 or fax (317) 572-4002.

Wiley also publishes its books in a variety of electronic formats. Some content that appears in print may not be available in electronic books. For more information about Wiley products, visit our web site at www.wiley.com.

Library of Congress Cataloging-in-Publication Data:

Anderson, Dave, 1961-
TKO hiring! : ten knockout strategies for recruiting, interviewing, and hiring great people / Dave Anderson.
p. cm.
Includes bibliographical references.
ISBN 978-0-470-17176-9 (pbk.)
1. Employees–Recruiting. 2. Employment interviewing. 3. Employee selection.
I. Title. II. Title: Recruiting, interviewing, and hiring great people.
HF5549.5.R44A525 2007
658.3'11–dc22
2007012356

10 9 8 7 6 5 4 3 2

Contents

Acknowledgments

Many thanks to my wife, Rhonda, who runs our business, covers my back, and keeps it all together as I jet around the world acting like I have a real job. Thanks also to the outstanding support staff and work partners in our California, Texas, and Virginia offices: You all are my dream team.

About the Author

Dave Anderson is president of LearnToLead, an international sales and leadership training organization. Dave has authored nine books, including the Wiley titles, *Up Your Business, If You Don't Make Waves You'll Drown* and *How to Deal with Difficult Customers*. He gives over 100 seminars and keynote speeches internationally each year and writes leadership columns for two national magazines. His website, www.learntolead.com has tens of thousands of subscribers in forty countries that enjoy an archive of over 400 free training articles. To inquire about having Dave speak to your group contact his Agoura Hills, California office at 800-519-8224 or 818-735-9503 (Intl). Dave is a member of the National Speaker's Association.

Introduction

With today's pace of business and as thin as you're spread as an employee, spouse, parent, and friend, you need high-impact information on how to improve your skills and elevate your organization; and you need it fast, without the hype, void of academics, and lacking complexity. This hiring edition of Wiley's TKO series is the answer.

This book has ten short Rounds that all get to the point and are filled with meaty strategies you can apply right away. In each Round you'll find Right Hook Rules—quotes and sound bites that reinforce what you're learning. You'll also relate to the TKO Tales that take real-life situations and use them as a context for how the principles you're learning can be applied. Finally, throughout each Round you'll find key Left Jab Laws that will be the catalysts to turning this book into an agent for change in your business.

Each Round in *TKO Hiring* concludes with a series of action-oriented Standing Eight-Count Questions and the book ends with a bullet-point summary of each Round's key points for quick reference and review. It's the *Cliff Notes* version of the manuscript.

A few words of caution concerning the TKO series: while the strategies presented in this book are easy to understand and apply, they're still hard work. Nonetheless, anything worthwhile is worth breaking a sweat for and the TKO format will make the hard work you have ahead of you more doable, enjoyable, and rewarding. If you've read my book, *Up Your Business: 7 Steps to Fix, Build, or Stretch Your Organization* (Wiley, 2003) then you will find many of the concepts in that work expanded on in this book. This will serve to review what you already know and take you to a deeper level of understanding and application of key strategies.

ROUND 1

Understand the Cost of Hiring Recklessly

Let's Start with Tough Talk

Have you ever given serious thought to the cost of hiring just one poor performer in your organization? I don't think you can quantify it with any degree of accuracy. Oh, I suppose you can quantify the cost of lost production between a top and bottom performer. That's the easy part. But how do you calculate the cost of broken momentum that the wrong people inflict on your team? You know what I mean by broken momentum: when dysfunctional employees create distractions and make messes that you have to clean up; or the extra time you must spend trying to motivate them or getting them up to speed. And what about the cost of lower morale? Nothing personal, but the fact is that poor performers lower the collective self-esteem of the whole team. Everyone, especially top performers, feels a bit cheapened and diminished when they're forced to share the workplace with those who can't cut it, don't do their share, or refuse to help the team reach their goals. As high as these costs are—lost production, broken momentum, and lower morale—I haven't even presented the highest cost yet that the wrong people inflict on your organization. Care to take a guess as to what it is? It is your own personal credibility as a leader. That's right. Your employees hear you talk big: "We're number one," "we have high standards," "not everyone can be one of us," and "this is a special place to work." But then they take a look around at the people you're allowing to remain in the workplace and, quite frankly, they're confused! "Number one?" "High standards?" "Special place to work?" they exclaim, "but Larry, Curly, and Mo still work here! The boss is talking right and walking left. He talks like a big dog but walks like a piss ant!" And make no mistake about it: You will lose the respect of the best when you don't deal effectively with the worst! Go ahead and try to lead effectively when you've lost the respect of the best. It's one tough task.

Right Hook RULE

People are not your greatest asset—the *right* people are. The wrong people are your greatest catastrophe. Mediocre people are your greatest drain on resources. We may all have equal value as human beings but we don't all bring equal value to the workplace.

They Hurt Worse When You're on a Roll

As costly as poor performers are, there are certain times when they hurt you far more than other times. Think of it this way: If you're the driver of a bus that is idling in neutral and one of your tires blows out, you will certainly have some damage but

Right Hook RULE

Train your managers how to recruit, interview, and hire. Hiring should not be a "learn-as-you-go/trial-and-error" experience.

> **TKO Tale**
>
> ***My Old Strategy***
>
> In my first management job, I received very little training for the first 18 months I was in charge of my department. Thus, I had no real hiring strategy. Well, I guess I did have a strategy, it just wasn't very effective. Let me share it with you: I'd wait until we were short-handed. Then, I'd run a dumb ad in the newspaper. The ad would bring in a bunch of morons and then I'd lower the bar so a few of them could clear it. I could then declare that we were fully staffed and had "coverage." Unfortunately, I've noticed that many managers have stolen my strategy over the years!

it won't be too drastic because you didn't have much speed or momentum. However, if your bus is humming along at ninety miles per hour and you have a blowout, you have a disaster on your hands. And that's the way it is with poor performers: They hurt your business most when you're rolling along because when you lose your momentum while traveling at a high speed it devastates your results and diminishes your culture. Bearing this fact in mind, please understand that the problem is compounded by the fact that it is precisely when we're doing well that we're also least likely to deal with the derelict, dismal, or depressed, thus ensuring they hang around long enough to bring us down right about the time we're at the top of our game.

The Toll Keeps Rising

One cost for hiring the wrong people that many leaders fail to consider is the price paid when they must divert their time, attention, and resources away from their best people in order to try and rehabilitate poor performers. When key employees are ignored they can become indifferent and lose their passion.

When you neglect your best people their attitudes become negative and their productivity declines. Since all business leaders and organizations have limited resources they are obligated to invest them where they gain the highest return, but this is made impossible when you are forced to engage in damage control and in plugging holes created by the lazy, the lousy, and the lost.

Misery on the Installment Plan

The American Management Association estimates it costs 3.5 times the annual salary of a departed employee to replace him or her. This includes time and resources spent in recruiting, interviewing, and hiring; lost production of the person while he or she gets up to speed; lost customers the departed employee takes with him or her; and lower productivity from other employees while they help the newcomer.

Yes, the cost of hiring recklessly is staggering! And it's not a one-time penalty either. It is misery on the installment plan! You and the rest of your team—and customers—pay for it over and over. This is why *TKO Hiring* will suggest to you that hiring should be an elimination process, not an inclusive process, and that the best time to fire is before you hire. Quite frankly, you must make it more difficult for the marginal, mediocre, and moronic to sneak on board your team.

In my book, *Up Your Business: 7 Steps to Fix, Build, or Stretch Your Organization* (Wiley, 2003), I titled the first chapter, "Always Remember: It's the People Stupid!" I inserted this not-so-subtle reminder to put in perspective that until you bring the right people on your team everything else is mostly irrelevant. After all, training, coaching, and motivating the wrong person brings little or no return on your time and energy. Think about it: Regardless of how brilliant your vision and strategy may be, you won't be able to attain it or execute it when burdened by bunglers. This makes hiring the highest leverage center of gravity on your job description. And that fact makes *TKO Hiring* your newest best friend.

Right Hook RULE

"Hire slow and fire fast."

—Harvey Mackay

Standing Eight-Count Questions

1. Do you have a written hiring policy for your organization?
2. What is the average annual salary in the job positions where you have the highest turnover?
3. What is the most noticeable cost that poor performers have on your organization: lower production; broken momentum; diminished team morale; lost personal credibility; other?
4. Do you normally wait until you're desperate before you look for employees to hire?
5. Does your organization have more voluntary or more involuntary turnover?
6. What can you do right away to begin making it tougher for the wrong people to get on board your team?
7. Do you personally get as involved as you should in the hiring process?
8. Do the hires that don't work out in your organization normally fail because of production issues or failing to live the values issues?

Notes

ROUND 2

Become a Proactive Recruiter

Opening Bell—You're not Unique!

In the past several years, I've averaged giving over one hundred speeches or seminars annually in thirteen different countries and nearly all fifty states. It seems that whether I'm in Atlanta, Los Angeles, New York, London, Palm Springs, or Podunk, I hear the same cop-out: "Dave, let me tell you about our area. Where we do business, we're a little different. We have a unique situation. There is a shortage of talented people in our particular area." Not that you've ever resorted to this type of whining, but in case you ever consider using it as an excuse, let me be the first to kick the crutch out from under you: There is no shortage of talented people in any particular area. The Creator didn't get ticked off at your area and stop putting talented people there. The fact is that the most productive, talented, and successful people already have jobs! They're not showing up at your place, hat in hand, looking for work. Thus, you must create a proactive recruiting strategy that addresses and attracts passive job candidates.

The Right Recruiting and Hiring Mindset

I want to give you a one-word recruiting strategy that sums up the essence of this Round: proactive. Quite frankly, if you want to build a great team of people you've got to stop sitting back waiting to be hunted and turn into a hunter. You must look in the right places and for the right traits; but *you* must look! You will never make great hiring decisions if you only look for people when you're desperate—when your back is against the wall and your vision is clouded by crisis.

Hiring is a lot like dating: As desperation rises, standards fall!

Focus on Performance Not Your Personal Preference

Before I get into the actual hiring strategies, I would like to suggest that to recruit the absolute best people for your organization you may have to subordinate your personal prejudices or biases to the good of the organization. Effective leaders care more about people's character, competence, and track record than their color, gender, or national origin. They also realize that driven, mature, older citizens shouldn't be eliminated because of an age bias. After all, would you rather hire a 55-year-old person that will give you 10 great years of performance or a 25-year-old fast talker that will provide you with 40 years of mediocrity?

Left Jab Laws for Proactive Recruiting

The worst time to recruit, interview, and hire is when you are desperate. You must be proactive and recruit year-round to build a pipeline of talent for your business. But you will never build this pipeline of talent if the only time you recruit, interview, or hire is when you need someone.

Develop a strategy for recruiting passive job candidates into your workplace: those workers already employed and productive in other jobs for other companies. These are the best candidates for the job, not those reading the want-ads. If you want to hire great people you must first talk to great people, and the best people are working.

The want ads are estimated to attract the bottom 30 percent of performers in any field. Thus, even if you manage to hire the best of that 30 percent employment pool, you're still just bringing on the best of the worst. In fact, most employment advertisements are worded in a way that appeals to mediocre candidates and turns off top performers.

Right Hook RULE

It's a safe bet to assume the best candidates for your business are not amongst the ranks of the unemployed.

You still should maintain some presence in the newspaper want-ads to attract people new to your area or people who are in the process of changing careers. But these ads should be only a small part of your overall recruiting effort and not the mainstay, and they should be worded in a manner that attracts people looking for challenges and scares off those just looking for a paycheck. Following are two sample ads that better explain this point.

Sample 1: Ad Attracting those Seeking Paychecks

Sales

"Thirty-year-old dealership is looking for motivated individuals to join our professional sales team. Prior sales experience helpful, but not necessary. Must possess great attitude and desire to succeed. We provide training, health and dental insurance, and 401k retirement plan. We offer a guaranteed monthly draw against commission. Must have high integrity and maintain a strong team concept."

This ad is typical and attracts anyone with a pulse. And you've coached the applicant to talk about what a great team player he or she is and fake a great attitude during the interview.

Sample 2: Ad Attracting those Seeking Challenges and Opportunities

Sales

"We're a fast-growing player in the automotive retail industry and need a self-starter who can build and manage his or her own business and complement our team of sales all-stars. If you've got the horsepower to take over this critical position, hit our high standards, and grow fast with our company, send in your resume or apply online at www.blahblahblah.com. Include a separate write-up describing your most significant team and individual accomplishments. We realize a compensation package needs to be very aggressive to continue to build our all-star team and we promote team members based on performance, not tenure.

One of the key differences between the two ads is the second one causes the candidate to sell him or herself, whereas the first ad does all the selling. When you sell a job too early or too soon, you cheapen it. The second ad will also scare off the slugs wanting to just get by and pick up an easy paycheck. On the other hand, it will intrigue top performers and get their juices flowing.

Right Hook RULE

An old adage declares, "be careful what you ask for because you're likely to get it." Thus, if your expectations are too low, people will tend to live down to them.

The second ad will not bring in as many job candidates and you should thank me for that because the people it does bring in will be of a higher quality, whom you've intrigued with the ad's wording. It will scare off the slugs just wanting to get by. They won't want any part of a workplace where it looks like there might be high expectations or where they might just be expected to break a sweat in order to keep their job.

Turn everyone in your organization into a recruiter and pay them well for bringing talented people into your workplace. Pay a bonus of at least $500 when an employee refers someone whom you hire. Pay half the bonus to the employee the day the new hire starts and the remainder after he or she has been there 90 days or so. Keep it simple. Don't make employees jump through hoops in order to claim their bonuses. In fact, you can bring great visibility and credibility to the bonus by paying it in a public meeting and creating some hype around it so that you leave a strong impression on everyone's mind that it's worth their effort to help recruit great people for your company.

Right Hook RULE

A significant and easy-to-collect-on recruitment bonus builds awareness among the rank and file that you are serious about surrounding them with great people and turns all employees into proactive talent scouts.

Market jobs to your customer base via direct mail or e-mail. These people are excellent passive job candidates. Your current customers are often ideal job prospects. They already know, like, and trust you and you have access to contact information that you can use to plant seeds for them to consider you for a career opportunity.

Attract passive job candidates through your web site with a "Join Our Team" icon. When someone clicks on it, the first thing they should see are employee testimonials from your happiest workers talking about how they love what they do and where they work. This function should also allow candidates to submit a five-line application online. All you are looking for on this application is contact information so you can call them for a preliminary phone interview. Applying online is a much less threatening way for great people to test the employment waters at your business rather than coming in and applying for a job in person. Respond to all online employment applicants quickly.

Managers should take more personal responsibility for recruiting and building their teams. It's their team, paycheck, and reputation. Thus, they are responsible for building it and not simply waiting for the company to run ads to fill the ranks. Hold managers accountable for actively recruiting people into their organizations. Make it a formal performance expectation. Eagle Calling Cards are an effective strategy to achieve this end.

Right Hook RULE

It is the lazy leader who places an ad in the newspaper and then waits for eagles to crash land at his or her doorstep.

Eagle Calling Cards

Eagle calling cards are another proactive strategy for planting seeds and building a pipeline of future employment prospects. These cards are the size of a business card and should say something similar to the following:

Front of Card

I noticed your great service today! We're always looking for winners to join our team. Please call me at 818-735-XXXX to discuss the opportunity in complete confidence, or apply online at www.xxxxxxxx.com.

Reverse of Card

A list of great things about your company, benefits, years in business, the great products you sell, training and promotion opportunities, and the like. You can also intrigue great people with features like: "Top Gun Club for our best performers; promotions based on performance, not tenure; flexible scheduling; our average salesperson made $XX last year."

Right Hook RULE

If you want to find great people you have to look in the right places. Eagles and turkeys don't eat the same food.

Create and Communicate a Compelling EVP

An EVP is your *employee value proposition*. It's what makes you different and better than other employers. When recruiting great people you must be able to recite your EVP quickly and concisely. Unfortunately, most companies are more alike than they are different: the same type of benefits, vacation policies, and so on. An EVP goes beyond those matters and may include things similar to what you have written on your Eagle Calling Card: "We have a special club for our top performers; promotions are based on performance and not on tenure; 90 percent of our managers have been promoted from within; we've never had a layoff; and we provide leadership mentoring programs for qualified employees."

TKO Tale

The Steakhouse Superstar

An automotive dealer client in New York treated me to dinner at the Buffalo Chop House. A group of ten of us had an incredible meal and a great time, and also managed to do a bit of recruiting at the same time. After being seated it became obvious that our waiter that night was something special. Sporting a contagious attitude and highly developed skills he quickly up-sold the entire table on the appetizers we ordered and on the bottle of wine as well. He had us laughing at his jokes and delivered fast and efficient service the entire night. Looking around, we noticed that he took just as good care of the other four tables he had that evening. I asked my client if he had his "Eagle Calling Cards" with him and suggested that this young man would make a great addition to his sales team. Joe gave the waiter the card, quickly recited his EVP, and planted a seed about how great the car business was and, within 60 days, this successful, employed, passive job candidate decided to change careers and go to work at Joe's dealership. While the average car salesperson sells between eight to ten cars per month, this new hire sold fourteen his first month and twenty his second month in the business. He went on to become a real star and what is most important to realize is that there is no way my client would have ever hired this gentleman through a conventional means like the want-ads because this fellow wasn't reading them. He wasn't looking. A proactive recruiter with a better offer simply came his way.

Right Hook RULE

You will occasionally hire a great person from the classified ads, but what you have to sift through in order to find him or her is absolutely exhausting. Overall, want-ads bring in a combination of the frustrated, the terminated, the curious, confused, and mystified! People barely doing enough to get by elsewhere and now they want to test their options at your place.

Use employment web sites to search for resumes of those looking for opportunities and to post your own job openings.

For far less than it normally costs to run a want-ad of a size that will get noticed, you can peruse hundreds of resumes and post your own job openings as well. Spend an hour or two of your time surfing the following sites and others like them so you too can elevate your hiring practices into this century. More and more great candidates and astute recruiters are drawn to the online aspect of recruiting. Don't be left out.

www.careerbuilder.com
www.monster.com

Sites like the two listed often charge you by the month to view the resumes posted there. You can look up potential candidates based on geography, job category, and compensation desired. The cost is reasonable considering what you would pay for a series of conventional advertisements in a mid- to large-sized newspaper. For instance, www.monster.com has specials that will let you roam its database for an entire month, in a one-hundred-mile radius, for $1,100–$1,200.

Debrief new hires for additional referrals. When you hire an outstanding employee debrief him or her to determine who else, where he or she worked, might be willing and able to join your team. Who was passed over for promotion? Who has had their pay cut or feels under-appreciated or micromanaged? Maximize your recruiting efforts by trying to turn one hire into two or three whenever it makes sense to do so.

TKO Tale

You are well advised to be cautious when hiring employees from competitors. First, make sure that you are doing enough to retain your own people in the event your competition decides to retaliate and raid your talent pool. Secondly, don't hire someone from a competitor who was just for the sake of "stealing an employee"; make certain that the person you're getting is an eagle!

I once had a manager boast to me that he had just "stolen" an employee from our competitor who was directly across the street from us. When I asked what sales numbers this new addition to our team had produced in his past job the manager gave me a number that was close to 30% lower than the national average for the position for which he was hired. To make a point, I asked my well-intentioned yet hasty protégé which day the trash was set out for pick up in his neighborhood. "Wednesday." I then asked if he ran across the street and stole his neighbor's trash after he placed it outside for pick up and brought it into his home. "Of course not." I concluded with a question that made my point well enough so that this up-and-coming leader never repeated the same careless mistake again: "If you don't bring your neighbor's trash from across the street into your house, why would you bring our competitor's discards from across the street into our business?

Raid talent pools when uncertainty reigns. If a business in your area has just been sold or has merged with another company, you can bet there is plenty of anxiety among the ranks of the employees there. Take advantage of this uncertainty by approaching the best people and trying to hire them into your organization.

Invest in radio advertisements. You're much more likely to make your case in front of qualified, passive job candidates if you run ads on the radio where they can hear them driving to and from their current jobs . . . and even while on the job someplace else.

Right Hook RULE

Don't hire "projects" in hopes that your business is the place where they will turn their lives around! You don't have the time or resources to re-circulate someone else's mediocrity.

No Magic Bullet

When it comes to building a better team through proactive recruiting there are no magic bullets. None of the strategies listed here will bring you a flood of eagle candidates overnight. But they will help you build a stronger team over time. If each of the primary ideas presented in this Round—eagle calling cards; re-wording your want-ads; e-mailing or direct mailing your customer base; turning your web site into a compelling recruitment post; paying recruitment bonuses more quickly; debriefing new hires; raiding talent pools when uncertainty reigns and using hiring web sites like those recommended—brought you only one great employee per year, I believe you'd agree they were well worth your time and effort to implement them.

Right Hook RULE

Nothing you can do will bring a higher return to your organization than finding the right people and putting them into the right places in your organization. In fact, until you accomplish this, everything else you do is somewhat irrelevant.

Standing Eight-Count Questions

1. Do you or your leaders currently rate proactive recruiting among one of the top responsibilities in your jobs?
2. On average, how many employees have your current managers personally recruited into their department? How about you?
3. What percentage of your recruiting effort is focused on want ads in newspapers?
4. What businesses in your area have high-quality, well-trained people where you could use the Eagle Calling Cards?
5. Is your web site currently a compelling recruitment post for passive job candidates? What more can you do to utilize it in this manner?
6. How effective has your organization been in garnering referrals from new hires?
7. Do you currently have a substantial enough recruitment bonus for employees who bring in referrals? Is it easy enough to collect this bonus?
8. When you do run an employment ad, do you word it in a way that attracts people looking for paychecks or does it appeal to those who are looking for opportunities?

Notes

ROUND 3

Create a Potent Interview Structure

Opening Bell

When I first began interviewing job candidates in my inaugural management job I was clueless. I didn't have any prestructured questions. I did most of the talking and wound up basically begging mediocre people to come to work for us. My interview style cheapened the position and turned off serious candidates who expected a tough interview. As a result I hired a lot of the wrong people and then spent a fortune training them with very little to show for my investment. Why? The losers I was bringing on board weren't giving us much to work with: no drive; lousy

> **Right Hook RULE**
>
> The number one cause of hiring errors is making emotional decisions during the interview. You need a structured process that keeps you logical and prohibits you from being influenced by personalities, personal biases, stereotypes, or appearances until you have been able to first establish job competence.

attitudes; questionable characters; and the same energy level required to power a toy boat in a bath tub. Fortunately, stupidity needn't be terminal and I've learned and practiced a much more effective interview strategy that I'll share with you next.

Rigorous is the Word

In an effort to keep things simple and focused, let me now present a one-word strategy that should embody the essence of your interviews: *rigorous*. Interviews need to be tougher. This is not a good-old–boy, get-acquainted session; nor is it a sales pitch; and neither should it be a casual conversation. An interview is a fact-finding expedition and it is one of the most important functions a manager performs. After all, there is so much at stake: production, momentum, morale, credibility, standards, and culture. You need a game plan that keeps you focused on looking for the right things, asking effective questions, and that will stop you from being duped or seduced by the things that don't matter.

Left Jab Laws for Creating a Potent Interview Structure

Before you interview someone for a position, define what a candidate must do to be successful in that job. To get great job performance, you must first define it. These objectives can also include your first 90 days or 12-month performance expectations for the job at hand.

Direct your interview to focus more on past accomplishments than past experience. This is because the best predictor of future performance is past performance. In other words, success leaves clues and so does failure. Because of this it's essential that you utilize behavioral-based questions that focus more on "do" (what they've done; accomplishments they have to their credit) over "have" (personality, experience, college degrees, a nice appearance, etc.). There are plenty of folks out there that "have" all these attributes and have failed to do much with them during the course of their lifetime.

Right Hook RULE

Winners tend to continue as winners unless the job or environment changes dramatically. On the other hand, losers tend to continue on as losers. If someone couldn't get the job done at place A or place B or place C, do you really think he or she is going to change in the moving van on the way to your business?

Frankly, top performers are turned off by questions that focus more on past experience than past accomplishments. Real winners want to talk about what they've done; not just what they have. Pretenders like to talk about what they have since in most cases they've never done much.

Right Hook RULE

Remember that while you may ultimately have to use intuition to finalize your hiring decision, intuition should be based on the right facts arrived at through careful, logical questioning—void of excess emotion.

Prestructure interview questions and stick to them during the interview process. Follow up the answers to weed out exaggeration. Since an interview is not a casual conversation you must turn it into a fact-finding expedition with questions that dig into past accomplishments.

Even if this is someone's first job, ask questions to determine what he or she accomplished when in school. Did he or she pay his or her own way by working three jobs? Did he or she show leadership through the participation in extra-curricular activities or community service projects? Did his or her grades improve or decline over the time he or she was in school?

Don't judge people strictly based on where they are in life. Determine what they had to overcome to reach to where they are now. To use a baseball analogy, the person who fouls off ten pitches before drawing a walk is preferred over the one who was born on third base and thinks he hit a triple.

Keep in mind that the number one cause of hiring errors is making emotional decisions during the hiring process. When you start to like someone too soon based on personality, appearance, or personal biases you stop assessing him or her because you want him or her to make the team. You begin to exaggerate the strengths and minimize the weaknesses. You are also likely to begin selling the job too soon. On the other hand if you don't like him or her for the mentioned reasons, you grow bored and start telling the person why he or she doesn't really want the job. Because you let your emotions get involved, you don't stick with someone long enough to see what he or she really brings to the table.

Right Hook RULE

Some job candidates are temporarily frozen by the glare of the interview spotlight. Writing them off too soon could cost you a great employee.

The number one cause of hiring mistakes comes from hiring emotionally: getting blown away by personalities, stereotypes, first impressions, or personal biases. It is estimated that 70% of the hiring decision is a result of presentation skills by the job candidate. Develop the discipline to stop making a first impression judgment until at least 30 minutes into the interview. It is estimated that more than 50% of hiring mistakes can be avoided if you'll avoid the "5-minute" first impression.

Right Hook RULE

If you like someone you tend to reduce performance standards. If you don't like him or her you don't care whether or not the person is competent. Asking the right questions helps you hire those good at doing the job, not just those good at getting the job. Many candidates have had plenty of practice at the latter.

A short telephone interview before the face-to-face interview will help you to overcome the power of the first visual impression: for better or worse. By speaking with someone over the phone, asking a few questions, and taking good notes, you'll be more objective when you actually lay eyes on the person.

Never get so seduced by presentation skills and personality that you forget that there is a significant difference between interview performance and job performance.

When you start to feel like you're going to enjoy the interview, you're in trouble. When several people interview the candidate and like him or her because of personality reasons, raise the caution flag!

TKO Tale

I once conducted a phone interview with a candidate so impressive that I couldn't wait to meet him . . . until I actually saw him. Frankly, Terry had the worst hairpiece I had ever seen in my life. His rug couldn't have been more obvious if Ali Baba had flown into my office on top of it. Without being hooked by the phone interview, I would have been so distracted that I couldn't have taken Terry seriously and, as a result, would have missed out on what turned out to be a star employee.

Throughout the interview process, remain the buyer and be tough—without being discourteous—on the job candidate. Top applicants expect a serious interview and the easier you make it to climb on board, the easier it is for employees to leave when they don't like the job any longer and the less they will respect the job. You can just hear the conversations in their heads: "If it was that easy to get a job here, this place can't be anything special. In fact, I'm not sure I'd want to work at a place that would hire someone like me so quickly." In the words of Emerson, "What people gain too easily they esteem too lightly."

On the other hand, when you make getting a job in your organization a grueling process—when people feel that they really have to make the cut and that not just anyone could work

Right Hook RULE

Enjoying the interview is an indicator that emotions are getting involved and you are losing your objectivity.

in your establishment—they will respect the job more when they get it and work very hard to live up to the higher standard.

Before you make a firm offer, test the waters with a question like, *"What would you think of an offer in the 'X' range?"* When asked hypothetically, the candidate is more likely to be open and reply honestly. Making a sample offer leaves you and the candidate "wiggle room" to maneuver so you create a win/win situation.

Throughout the interview process listen at least four times as much as you speak. The candidate is on trial, not you. Resist the temptation to talk too much during the interview. This is a fatal flaw.

Right Hook RULE

You cannot effectively evaluate another person if you're doing all the talking. The interview is not about you! It's about the job candidate.

Build your team around individual excellence, not the easy-to-manage or the harmonious applicant. Liking the person is not the first thing you should be concerned with. After all, there are plenty of likable losers in the workplace today. Your first concern should be to determine whether or not the person shares your values and is capable of doing the work. You'll find it easier to learn to like someone who is actually competent. Besides, what good does it do for you to have a group of friendly and harmonious bunglers wandering around all day who are incapable of getting the job done?

Keep highly developed leaders involved in the interview process. Top leaders have a better eye for talent. They will also make a better impression on the job candidate. Don't let untrained, lower-level leaders conduct interviews. These people are oftentimes intimidated by independent, aggressive, and talented job candidates. They tend to look for the "easy-to-manage" candidate who is no threat to their own egos or positions. Remember the words of Sir Arthur Conan Doyle: "Mediocrity knows nothing higher than itself, but talent instantly recognizes genius."

TKO Tale

I spent many childhood years growing up in a Texas neighborhood where I was a perennial team captain and my rival was a kid named Randy. For 6 years, Randy and I chose sides for football, baseball, and basketball. For those same 6 years my teams always lost and Randy's always won. As a manager in the making, I naturally blamed my team. However, as I grew older and wiser and began to reflect, the truth hit me: We'd lost for 6 straight years because I'd picked my friends while Randy had picked the best players. I'd chosen my brother, my neighbor, my best friend—all kids I knew I could get along with and control. Randy, however, picked the biggest, the fastest, and the meanest. I wanted harmony and he wanted to win. The truth was, though, that as we continually lost we had very little harmony on the team. On the other hand, Randy's victory streak caused his team to bond like brothers. Winning has a way of doing that when a good coach is at the helm.

Have candidates run the gauntlet by requiring several highly qualified interviewers to assess the job candidate and then get together to share feedback and compare notes. Let me repeat: several *highly* qualified interviewers and not just whoever happens to have some free time on their hands. However, do not vote on whether or not to bring the candidate on board. This decision should be made and owned by the employee's direct supervisor.

After you make an employment offer, plant seeds to fend off a counter offer from a current employer. Use a script similar to this one:

Right Hook RULE

If you are a leader and you believe you're too busy to interview the people joining your team, your priorities are horribly misguided. In fact, you don't have a clue as to what your real job is.

"When you tell your current employer you are leaving, be prepared for a counter offer and how you'll handle it. When employees accept counter offers the relationship they have with their bosses from that point on are weakened. They become suspect and are never trusted at the same level they once were. You should also consider whether or not waiting until you announce you're leaving before getting serious about valuing you as an employee is an acceptable tactic to retain your talents."

Throughout the interview process, remind the candidate of the competition. Say something like:

"While we are continuing to speak with several strong candidates, we feel you would make a solid contribution to our team. At this point, what are your feelings or concerns about the position being offered?"

Right Hook RULE

Marc Andreessen of Netscape's "Rule of Crappy People": Bad managers tend to hire very, very bad employees because they're threatened by anybody who is anywhere as good as they are.

Don't focus on the exception when hiring; focus on the rule. Too many leaders are enamored with the dark horse, the underdog. Resist the temptation to think the long-shot candidate in front of you is the next "Rocky" or "Rudy" of your business. You cannot build a team of eagles around potential exceptions.

Throughout the interview process it's important to remember that while you can teach skills and knowledge, you can't teach talent, attitude, drive, or personality. You must hire those traits in. That's why predictive testing should be mandatory as it helps you determine whether the person has the things you are unable to teach him or her. More about this is in Round six.

Right Hook RULE

When hiring, you cannot afford to give the benefit of the doubt. It indicates you are already making excuses for the job candidate and he or she hasn't even joined your team yet!

Right Hook RULE

All the training, motivating, and coaching in the world will not be enough to turn a person not fit for the work into to a solid performer. Taking a stronger whip to a dead horse will not move it.

Standing Eight-Count Questions

1. Do you keep highly developed and well-trained interviewers involved in the interview process?
2. Do your interviews focus more on past experience or past accomplishments?
3. Do you discipline yourself to keep your emotions out of the interview process and not decide to like or dislike the candidate too soon?
4. Do you conduct phone interviews before the actual in-person interview?
5. Are your interviews tough or have they been too casual?
6. Do you find yourself doing too much of the selling in an interview?
7. Do you give employment candidates with little proven track record too much benefit of the doubt?
8. Are your interview questions prestructured in writing or do you improvise during the interview?

Notes

ROUND 4

Ask Tough Interview Questions

Opening Bell

In my workshops, I give examples of how some of the most common interview questions, that sound good at the outset, offer little insight into the candidate's track record or job competence. To make the point, I use a couple of extreme scenarios that generate lots of laughs but, more importantly, drive my point home.

For instance, if you ask someone applying for a sales position, "Tell me about your strengths?", what is likely to be his or her reflexive, pat answer to this inquiry? Most likely the candidate will reply, "I'm a people person. People really like me and I get along well with all kinds of people." I then point out that Hannibal Lechter could be considered a people person, but he is probably not someone you'd want waiting on your customers. Another oftentimes useless question to ask someone is, "Tell me about your weaknesses." In all honesty, do you really think that anyone is going to make a heartfelt confession for you? Could you imagine someone saying, "Well, my biggest weakness is that I'm a procrastinator. I can't even manage to get up most mornings. The alarm goes off and I dream that I get up but I don't. In fact, I'm surprised I'm even here today." Or how about, "This is just between you and me, right? Well, I've been working on this weakness for a long time and I just about have it beat. . . . but I'm a thief. I steal food, money, and pens. By the way, here's your wristwatch back. And one more confession . . . I have a cocaine habit but really I consider that a strength since it motivates me to make a lot of money."

If you want meaningful answers you must ask meaningful questions.

Be a "Smart Asker"

Now that you've assumed the right mindset and created a potent interview structure to evaluate the candidate, it's time to ask the right questions. Remember that this is very important business so you must put your game face on. Be polite but remain serious. There is a lot at stake. Keep in mind that you are, first and foremost, trying to determine job competence and the level of past accomplishments a potential new hire may bring to the table. Thus, craft your questions in a way that brings forth answers that will lend insight into this objective. The questions I'm providing you are a great start but you may certainly add your own.

It's Crunch Time

Before you actually begin asking the questions, put yourself in a more psychologically favorable position by setting the stage in your favor. As the interviewer, in less than 3 minutes, introduce yourself, state your title and job duties, give a quick overview of the company, and give a compelling vision and description of the job being offered. Most interviewers wait until the end of the interview to explain about their company. Psychologically, this is a crucial time of the interview because the last person "selling" is at a disadvantage. You want to do your "selling" up front and then throughout the rest of the interview stay in the driver's seat by having the candidate sell you. Once this ground work has been laid, you can immediately follow up with, "*Tell me how your background has prepared you for this position.*" Then follow up with these inquiries.

1. Give me an overview of your current job and describe for me the most significant accomplishment you've achieved there.

I can't think of a question that will tell you more about someone's past performance and level of thinking than when you ask him or her to describe what he or she believes is the most significant thing he or she has accomplished at work. Ask this same question for the past several jobs and determine if the most significant accomplishment is becoming more or less impressive.

TKO Tale

I can recall interviewing a sales candidate while I managed an automotive dealership in Texas. When I asked him the "most significant accomplishment" question he replied, "I guess that my biggest achievement was last April when I sold seven cars." Bearing in mind that the national average units sold by a car salesperson is ten units, I had to restrain myself from looking at my watch and declaring, "Wow! We're all out of time. The door is right behind you. Go home and wait by the phone. If it doesn't ring, it's me." Needless to say, this interview didn't last very long. After all, if the best someone has ever done equates to 30% worse than average it makes the hiring decision quite simple.

2. One of our objectives is XXX (name an actual objective for the job). Name for me the most relevant experience you've had achieving something similar in other jobs?

This helps you determine how close they've ever come to doing what you're going to need them to accomplish.

3. One of our objectives is XYZ. If you get the job, how will you go about accomplishing this?

This is a trick question. A poor candidate will respond to this question by quickly rattling off one-size-fits-all solutions without asking you questions about how you're currently doing things in your organization. A great candidate will slow you down a bit here and diagnose your organization by asking you a few questions before he or she prescribes solutions.

4. We expect everyone working for us to make some mistakes and cost us some money during their employment. Can you describe for me some of the most significant mistakes you've made in prior jobs and what you learned from them?

This question helps determine if the candidate is (1) honest, because we've all made mistakes and (2) willing to take chances and get out of the box by trying new things.

5. Can you describe for me some of the books, tapes, and DVDs in your personal-development library at home?

The answer to this question will help reveal whether or not the candidate is a know-it-all who has stopped learning about his or her business and no longer sees the value of self-improvement or upgrading his or her skills. A great candidate is someone who sees the value of growth, continues to work on him or herself, and realizes there is still a lot to learn.

6. Tell me about one of the best and one of the worst hires you made as a manager. Why would you say things worked out as they did in each case? Start with the best hire.

The answer to this question will speak volumes about the candidate's own knowledge of this crucial job function and help reveal whether or not he or she takes credit for the good while passing the buck for the bad.

7. Describe for me your five biggest wins in any job or combination of jobs.

The candidate's reply will help you determine a candidate's level of thinking because what he or she believes are "big wins" may not even come close to cutting it in your organization.

What Not *to Ask*

While this is not a complete list of questions that can get you into trouble, it's a pretty good start. Check with your attorney or HR department for additional questions you may wish to add to this "don't ask" list.

1. You cannot ask about a candidate's age or tricky questions that can reveal it such as, "when did you graduate high school?"
2. Stay away from family matters or issues involving kids, a spouse, or martial status. If a candidate brings up this topic it's all right for you to respond, but don't pry.
3. Avoid questions pertaining to what someone does in his or her off time as these may progress into discussions of clubs he or she belongs to, religion, or political tendencies.
4. You can ask about convictions but not about arrests since an arrest is not the same thing as a conviction.

Follow the general rule to avoid personal questions and ask performance questions instead and you'll stay out of legal trouble and find out what is most relevant all at the same time.

Right Hook RULE

It is not necessary to ask a large volume of questions during the interview. What is important is that you ask a handful of the right questions and then dig deep for specifics.

Left Jab Laws

When the candidate replies, don't accept general answers. Dig deep for specifics: how many, what did you learn, what worked and what didn't, what changes did you implement, what resistance did you have to overcome, what would you do differently if you did it over, and the like. The deeper you dig the more exaggeration you will weed out and the clearer picture you'll get of the person's ability and character.

In addition to the suggested interview questions previously listed, ask a very stressful question or two to see how the candidate responds.

I can't think of too many positions in any organization where the ability to handle stress well would not be essential. Unfortunately, you wind up finding out the hard way that someone cannot do this . . . right after he or she blows up at a customer or crumbles under the pressure of team competition or quotas. How can you determine whether or not someone can handle a stressful situation in an interview? Ask a stressful question—something that is a bit provocative and unexpected. An effective technique is to wait until you're halfway through the interview, pause, look the candidate in the eye, and ask respectfully, but sincerely, "how would you feel if I told you the interview wasn't going very well at this point?" Then watch how the person responds. Some of them will blame you with remarks like, "You haven't even given me a chance," or "You're not asking the right questions," and the like. This tells you a lot about the person. They are defensive, prideful, or might have trouble taking responsibility. On the other hand, when someone responds with, "I'm sorry to hear that. What am I missing?" this is an indicator of the willingness to hold oneself accountable. Naturally, if the interview is going well, you want to tell the person that by saying, "Actually, I feel the interview is going well. I was just curious as to how you'd respond if I told you it was not."

If this sounds too harsh to you then please remember all that is at stake when you make a hiring decision and resolve to do whatever you can to ensure you are not making a hiring error. And let me paraphrase what C.S. Lewis said about the power of provocative, unexpected questions: If you have rats in the cellar, you're more likely to see them if you go down suddenly, before they have a chance to hide. The suddenness of your approach doesn't create the rats. It merely reveals those that already exist. The same goes when you ask a sudden, unexpected question. It doesn't create a defensive, sarcastic, irritable person. It merely reveals the defensive, sarcastic, irritable person seated in front of you.

In closing out these strategies on creating a rigorous interview process, keep this in mind: You can either devote your time and energy to following these steps and proactively building a team of eagles or you can devote your time and energy continually pushing the wrong people to do the right things, or, equally as bad, doing more of the work yourself since you don't have the right people around to help shoulder the burden.

Standing Eight-Count Questions

1. Are the interview questions you've asked in the past behavioral based?
2. Which behavioral-based questions can you add to those already given?
3. On average, how many follow-up questions do you ask in order to weed out exaggeration after a candidate replies?
4. Do your interviews do a good-enough job in determining whether or not a potential hire can handle stress?
5. Do you set the tone for the interview by doing your "selling" briefly and up front and then putting the candidate on trial for the remainder of the interview?
6. Do you and your managers avoid the "don't ask" questions during an interview? Which others can you add to the prohibited list?
7. Have your past interviews focused more on a large volume of questions or a more specific and narrow group of questions with heavy follow up?
8. What are the first three steps you will take to improve the way you and your other managers interview?

Notes

ROUND 5

Effectively Check References

Opening Bell

Once while checking a reference for an applicant I was gleaning very little useful information from his guarded boss when I asked, "I know that I've taken too much of your time already so let me just ask you that if you had to rate John Smith on a scale of one to ten as an employee, where would you put him?" He answered, "a seven." Then when he replied to my next question, "What would he have had to do to be considered as an eight?" with "not call in sick so often," it made not hiring this particular candidate an easier decision. In addition to the question I asked, here are a few other strategies:

> **Right Hook RULE**
>
> When asking reference questions you have everything to gain and nothing to lose so ask away . . . but ask with finesse.

Let the Games Begin

This Round is short but vital because with ever-changing laws and the fear of lawsuits, it's become increasingly more difficult to learn much about a job candidate when checking references. Thus, you must get out of the box and become more creative. When you are checking references use the following strategies to help dig out the truth concerning the applicant. As always, in today's litigious society you are well advised to check with both your legal counsel and HR department to ensure that the strategies in this Round comply with your own corporate policies as well as always-changing state and federal laws.

Left Jab Laws

Check with subordinates of the person being considered. Find out the names of these people during the interview and then call them. They are often more open and less guarded in what they tell you. Yes, you might get some sour grapes from someone with an axe to grind, but it's up to you to sift this out.

Use the following script when setting the tone for reference checking:

"Mr. Jones, since the law prohibits us from discussing any personal issues concerning Bob Smith, let's focus on performance issues if that's all right with you."

Then delve into performance-based questions since you have just lowered defenses and legitimized your approach.

Use questions like the following to further determine what you can find out about a job applicant. The former employer may or may not be of much help here, but until you ask you'll never know for sure.

1. When did (name) work for your company? Could you confirm starting and ending employment dates? When did he/she leave the company?
2. Why did (name) leave the company?
3. What was her/his starting and ending salary?
4. What was her/his position? Can you describe the job responsibilities?
5. Could I briefly review (name's) resume? Does the job title and job description match the position that (name) held?

6. Did (name) miss a lot of work? Was s/he frequently late? Were there any issues you are aware of that impacted her/his job performance?
7. Did s/he get along well with management and coworkers?
8. Was (name) promoted while with your company?
9. Did (name) supervise other employees? How effectively? If I spoke to those employees, how do you think they would describe (name's) management style?
10. How did (name) handle conflict? How about pressure? Stress?
11. Did you evaluate (name's) performance? Can you describe his/her strong and weak points? Which areas did the review point out as those most needing improvement?
12. What was (name's) biggest accomplishment while working for your company?
13. Would you rehire (name) if the opportunity arose?
14. Can you describe this person's effectiveness working as a member of a team?
15. On a scale of one to ten, where would you rank (name's) performance as an employee? Then raise the number one digit over what the employer gave you and ask the following: "What could Mr. Smith have done to raise his ranking to a XXX."
16. Is there anything I haven't asked that you would like to share with me?

Use the following script as your last reference-checking question:

"Mr. Jones, if you could whisper one piece of advice into Bob Smith's ear to help him be successful in his next job, what would you tell him?"

Another strategy is when you are concluding the interview and reviewing the references given on the application, to ask the candidate:

"Could you provide one additional personal and job reference for me who is not listed here?"

Naturally, the candidate will list his or her best references first so in this manner you get one that may not have been coached on what to say if you call.

Record detailed notes of your conversation when checking references and keep them in the employee's file.

Check personal references as well as employment references. Check for signs of character issues during your inquiry. The people you're asking are likely to be far less schooled on what they can or cannot say so these calls can bring forth great fruit. Keep in mind that if a personal reference is reluctant to tell you much, it's probably not because they don't want to help their friend/relative but because they're covering for him or her. Thus, you must also pay attention to what "isn't" being said.

If you run a credit report on a prospective employee there is a very good chance that former employers will be listed as inquiries on that report. This may help you determine where else the employee has worked and compare it against what he or she listed on his or her resume as well as discover what other companies he or she has recently applied to work at since the date of the inquiry will be listed on the report. Check their MySpace or Facebook web page for more insight into their habits, character, and associations.

Right Hook RULE

Remember that after you've gone through all this effort to hire the right candidate and are still not sure as to whether or not you should bring him or her on board: when in doubt, keep looking. A bird in the hand is not better than two in the bush if it's the wrong bird!

Standing Eight-Count Questions

1. Do you ask for one additional reference that the candidate has not listed?
2. When you check references do you tell the former employer that you'd like to focus on performance rather than personal issues?
3. Have you ever checked with the subordinate of an applicant when checking references?
4. Do you check personal references as well as those from former employers?
5. How heavily do the answers you get from references weigh on your decision to hire a candidate?
6. If you get a negative reference are you inclined to give the candidate the benefit of the doubt because you liked him or her?
7. Do you have an HR department that checks references or is this left up to the individual manager for whom the employee will be working? HR normally is more objective.
8. Do you take detailed notes during the employee reference check and keep the notes in the employee's file?

Notes

ROUND 6

How to Use Predictive Testing Hiring Profiles

Opening Bell

The Myth of "Unlimited Potential"

Early in my career, I had a well-intentioned but ill-informed boss who shared the following hiring advice: "Anderson, everyone has unlimited potential. Your job as a leader is to bring it out of them. If you train, coach, and learn to motivate your people, you can take twos and turn them into tens." This sounded good to me and I felt up to the challenge. So, while conducting an interview, I would be drawn to the friendly candidates with a good attitude and decent appearance even though they hadn't really ever done much in any job or in life overall. In my mind, they didn't have any real baggage so, even though they didn't have any real strengths either, I felt that with our product and my training and leadership, I could take these twos and turn them into tens. But I soon found that I couldn't. Oh, I tried. I would train them, give them feedback, motivate them, and throw more and more money at them to get them moving but I couldn't get them much better. In fact, I was lucky to turn a two into a four, much less a ten. As a result, I beat myself up pretty bad. I must be a lousy leader, trainer, and coach. After all, these people had unlimited potential, why couldn't I bring it out of them?

Well, with much study, research, and many conversations with people wiser than myself, I learned the truth about "unlimited potential." Everyone does have unlimited potential at *something*. But, obviously, everyone can't have unlimited potential at everything or we'd all be just alike. What I discovered was that human beings have unlimited potential in areas where they are talented—gifted, in an area of their natural strength. That doesn't mean we can't get somewhat better in areas where we don't have these things. It just means that we'll probably never be great in these areas because excellence is impossible without talent. Talent has been described as God's gift to you to make the world a better place. Some people have a talent for numbers; for art; for singing; fixing things; building things; communicating and the like. These talents must still be developed, but they are the seeds to greatness.

After further study, I learned that there were some things you can teach people and some that you cannot. It is essential that you fully understand the differences when you're hiring people or else you can expect to waste countless hours and resources trying to draw something out of someone that doesn't exist. Here are the facts: You can teach skills and knowledge. But you can't teach talent, drive, attitude, character, or a high energy level. In other words, you cannot put in what was left out. You can only draw out what was left in! If these traits are important to you, you'll have to hire them in. The natural question that now comes up is, "how do you know if someone has these things?" While there is no sure way to tell, there are specific tasks you can perform that certainly stack the odds in your favor. The first is to examine his or her track record as recommended in Round three. After all, a track record of someone's work history and life overall will leave clear clues as to the existence—or lack—of talent, drive, attitude, character, or a high energy level. The second task is to use a pre-employment assessment. These tools have become quite accurate in assessing talent. They're not perfect, but the right test will give you clear insight into whether or not the person is giving you something to work with.

Right Hook RULE

While talent is only potential, it is a great head start. Training someone in a job for which he or she has no talent is simply performing a type of damage control. You can prop him or her up to a degree with techniques, but he or she will never be great at what you need him or her to do if he or she lacks the unteachables.

Learn to Read Their Mail

Regardless of whether you currently use some type of pre-employment assessment or profile, this Round will help you use it more wisely or encourage you to begin using them to make all hiring decisions. There are dozens of different types of tests so it's best to do some research to determine which will work best for you. The guidelines in this section will give you a head start toward that end.

Left Jab Laws

Use predictive testing to help you determine whether someone has a talent for the job. Predictive testing helps you determine whether or not the person is bringing to the table the traits you cannot teach him or her.

Keep in mind that even if someone scores well on your pre-employment test you must delve deep into their track record to see what he or she has done with their potential because talent, while a great head start, is still just potential. It is no guarantee of great performance.

Come to grips with the fact that you cannot teach talent. If talent could be taught, there would be hundreds of Michael Jordan's, Robert DeNiro's, Eric Clapton's, and Wayne Gretzky's. You cannot train people to use what they don't have! And unless you are God who can bestow the gift of talent, you'll need to give up on this endeavor.

Face the reality that you cannot teach drive. Drive is an inside job. You cannot make someone want it.

From time to time I have people approach me at seminars and lament, "I just don't have any drive. What can I do?" I startle them when I reply, "I'm very sorry but there's nothing I can do for you. Please get away from me before I catch what you've got! You must give the universe something to work with!"

Accept that you can't teach people attitude. Yes, you may be able to alter their mood a bit from day to day but you cannot change the prevailing way in which they see the world.

Resign yourself to the reality that you are unable to teach employees character. By the time they reach the workplace, their character has long-ago been formed. While it is true that people can change themselves in areas of character, you cannot change them.

Right Hook RULE

Unfortunately, there are no 3-day character clinics where you can round up all the liars, cheats, and thieves and send them away for a long weekend and get them back all cleaned up.

You'll also need to give up on the notion of teaching employees how to have a high energy level.

Right Hook RULE

You may be able to inspire a fear-based adrenaline rush from time to time but you cannot consistently affect the energy level of a snail-paced employee.

Using the Profiles

As mentioned earlier, you'll need to do some research into companies offering these testing instruments and choose one that best serves your needs. I suggest you focus on those that will help determine whether or not the candidate has the traits like those mentioned in this section that cannot be taught. It is also helpful to use a company that offers the tests online so you get instant results. I believe that the Winslow Research Institute does the best job in both these areas; so much so that I have partnered with them to assist our clients with their hiring practices. Winslow profiles have been around for 40 years and are used by organizations ranging from professional sports teams to Fortune 200 companies. You can reach the folks at Winslow at 804-798-3355.

Another company that provides quality and highly regarded assessments is the Caliper Corporation out of Princeton, New Jersey. In fact, some of the Caliper principals wrote a book that I highly recommend: *How to Hire and Develop Your Next Top Performer* (McGraw Hill, 2001) by Herb Greenberg, Harold Weinstein, and Patrick Sweeney. While you're building your hiring library, get *Hire with Your Head* (John Wiley & Sons, 1998) by Lou Adler. It's an outstanding work that expands more deeply on many of the concepts in this book.

In addition to helping you eliminate hiring errors, assessments provide a valuable coaching tool if you do hire the employee as they point out strengths to be built upon and weaknesses to address as well.

Expense or Investment?

The major objection to using prehiring assessments is that they are "another expense." Yes, they will cost some money, but don't forget the cost of hiring recklessly and bringing on board the wrong person! The assessment is a very cost-effective form of insurance that protects you from "human" disasters known as poor performers or outright crooks.

Thus far in your journey to hire great people we've talked about a lot of basic disciplines. They don't require rocket science calculus but they do require tenacity. In fact, they're a lot of work. Proactive recruiting, changing your website, passing out Eagle Calling Cards, sending out mailers, paying recruitment bonuses, rigorous interviews with multiple people, preemployment testing, and more. But you can either pay the price up front to bring great people on board, or pay a greater price in the future for hiring recklessly. It is your choice, so choose well.

Right Hook RULE

Don't get so caught up with the cost of doing something that you fail to consider the cost for neglecting it.

Standing Eight-Count Questions

1. Does the pre-employment test you currently use determine the five unteachables listed in this Round?
2. Which of your employees is currently mis-employed in a position for which they are not fitted talentwise?
3. Who on your team has raw talent that has not yet been developed? What will you do to help draw it out of him or her?
4. In the past, when a job applicant has scored well on the pre-employment test, did you still dig into his or her track record to determine what, if anything, he or she had done during his or her career with the talent he or she showed to have?
5. Does your organization consider the costs involved with pre-employment as an expense or as an investment?
6. If someone scores poorly on your pre-employment test for a particular job, does the assessment you use currently give suggestions for which position he or she may be better suited?
7. In the past, have you allowed prospective employees who take a test but don't work out to discourage you from using them on other job candidates?
8. Are people able to take your current pre-employment assessments online?

Notes

ROUND 7

How to Get New Hires Off to a Great Start

Opening Bell

In some of my seminars, I ask attendees to estimate the amount of time it takes to hire a new employee and get him or her up to speed from the moment they begin recruiting, through the interview and testing stage, past the training phase, and up to a point where the employee is working at a level of satisfactory output. The most common answers range from 90 to 180 days. I then ask them to estimate the cost of this process: from recruiting and training costs; management time in doing these tasks; production loss while the new employee gets up to speed; and the like. Depending on the actual position the most common answers range from $20,000 to $100,000. I then relate a true story of when I was hired to go on premise to consult with a large automotive dealership. The general manager asked me to spend some time evaluating a new manager recently hired and determine if I felt they had made a mistake. According to the G.M., the new guy just didn't seem to "get it."

After spending nearly 2 hours questioning and conversing with the questionable candidate I reported that I felt they had a great prospective employee. The problem was that expectations had never been clearly defined; he had received no orientation or training upon hiring and was, in a nutshell, lost. I recommended that if a mentor could be assigned for a week or two to show this high-potential around that I felt confident he'd find his rhythm quickly and quickly become a productive contributor. The general manager shook his head and replied that, "Dave, we're a high-powered organization and we expect people that work here to be able to hit the ground running. We don't have 2 weeks to get him situated. We don't have 2 days; in fact we would barely have 2 hours."

I quickly did the math in my head: 90 to 180 days to get a replacement for this guy up to speed and a cost of tens of thousands of dollars and they can't find 2 weeks, 2 days, or 2 hours to get him going? If ignorance truly is bliss, I knew I had just met the happiest general manager in the industry.

Right Hook RULE

If you have good people and don't invest in them you deserve to lose them. In fact, you probably will. And if they do stay you don't deserve to get great results from them because you're looking for the prize without paying the price.

It's Your Turn to Make a Good First Impression

Think about how foolish it is to work hard to find and hire a great employee and then throw him or her into the fray of your business with a welcoming handshake, 1 day of completing paperwork, 2 days of orientation, little or no training, and best wishes for a successful career. This unfortunate practice is both common and costly. Employees begin deciding quickly whether or not they made the right decision in agreeing to work in your firm and will mentally check-out of your business long before they physically exit in search of a "real" company. You must put as much effort into maximizing employees' first 90 days with your company as you do when hiring them in the first place. In fact, within the first 9 hours, many new hires have gained irreversible negative impressions and become so disillusioned that their enthusiasm wilts faster than willpower at a Krispy Kreme counter.

Right Hook RULE

The challenge to retain talented people should keep every great leader awake at night.

Left Jab Laws: Getting New Hires Off to a Great Start

Throwing new hires into the frays of their jobs without proper orientation and culture inculcation is a leadership failure. After hiring the wrong person at the outset or having an ineffective manager under which an employee suffers, sloppy on-boarding processes are the primary culprit for poor employee retention.

While it often takes 90 days to gain a clear picture of how someone will do in his or her position; the first 30 days are the most essential to setting the stage for productive employment. To create even more urgency to get new hires off to a good start, realize that HR studies show that within the first 2 weeks the employee has already made up his or her mind that the workplace is either what was expected or have decided to continue with the job search—while continuing to collect your paychecks. Very early on new employees begin to sense that their basic needs for survival either will or will not be met at a particular job and they will then react accordingly. I once conducted a 45-minute tele-seminar for clients on the topic of getting new hires off to a great start and the feedback was such that I felt I should share the information on a broader basis and, as a result, have decided to include it in this book.

Following are seven steps to incorporate into your current on-boarding process to get employees off to a fast and productive start and improve your retention of them for the long haul.

Right Hook RULE

The great thing about a fast start is that you never have to recover from it.

1. Highly structure their first day. On their first day of employment they are both excited and nervous. Without structure, their excitement will wane and their nervousness may turn to negativity. To pull this off, the following should take place:

The direct supervisor should take a primary role in assuring that the new-hires' first day is busy, focused, and productive. Don't "hand off" the new hires to a subordinate on the first day. As their boss, you should take an active leadership role in guiding them through one day on the job.

Use a checklist with the most vital tasks to be accomplished that day. Your checklist should contain things like: a tour of the business; review of performance, and behavioral expectations; a detailed explanation of the pay plan; and so on. Each point on the checklist should be signed-off on by the employee and supervisor and given to Human Resources for placement in the employee's file.

If you structure the first day right, there will be no real time for training. There will be plenty of time for training in upcoming days. The first day should be primarily focused on getting the employees acquainted with others, comfortable with their surroundings, and familiar with procedures and policies. Once these basic needs of security and safety are met, the employees are ready to move on to developing competencies and contributing to the team.

2. Set forth training objectives for the next 30 days so the employee knows up front what he or she is expected to learn. You may also assign a mentor to help with the designated areas. For instance, in sales, this may mean that in 30 days you will teach and expect the salesperson to learn: a meet and greet; appointment phone script; key investigative questions; a referral script; and the like. Even if the employee has experience in your industry it is important that you teach him or her to do things your way. At the end of 30 days test the person on the assigned training tasks. Put these expectations in writing and have the employee sign-off on them.

Right Hook RULE

Good people will try hard to hit a standard if they clearly understand what it is. But it's hard for people to become focused and inspired if where they're headed is covered in fog.

3. Establish product knowledge goals for the first 30 days. You should focus your energies on your best-selling products first. You may wish to assign the salesperson one or two "products of the week" to learn about in-depth. Assign a mentor to do presentations on these products with the new employee and let the person know you will test him or her on these products at the end of a prescribed period of time. If the person is not in sales, customize this point so he or she learns the most vital aspects of the job: mastering

Right Hook RULE

Ambiguity is the enemy of accountability.

certain reports, computer functions, and so forth. These tasks set up a benchmark for accountability in the future.

4. Go over company core values, mission, vision, job description, and performance expectations. It is always best if these can be put in writing in the company handbook. Handbook? Yes, hopefully you have an employee handbook that outlines everything from dress code to days off and vacation policies. It's much more effective if you can go over the highlights of this book with the new hires rather than just tossing it to them and asking them to read it later. People must understand exactly what is expected of them and what they can expect from you.

If you would like to review sample job descriptions for ideas on creating your own, go to an Internet search engine and type in "Job descriptions" and you'll discover many sites that can be of help to you in this regard. In fact, if you work in a small organization without a Human Resources department, you can find many helpful forms that are valid in all fifty states: vacation requests, employment applications, conduct write-up forms, and dozens more. One is the Adams Personnel Forms CD available in most office supply stores like Staples, Office Depot, or Office Max.

Right Hook RULE

"It's hard to be aggressive when you're confused."

—Vince Lombardi

5. Some time during the first 2 to 3 days, have a senior manager or owner (if you're a small- to mid-sized firm) meet with the new hires to give them some history of the company. When shared, these stories become a bonding point between veteran and new employees.
6. Assign and pay a mentor to help the new employees master the tasks you've given. This person should be someone with a positive attitude and who shares the company values. Depending on your pay scales, $250 per month or so is a good place to start when paying a mentor.
7. Personally meet with the new employees at least once weekly during the first month to formally gauge progress, make yourself available for questions, and reinforce their sense of belonging into the organization. You cannot meet with a person once the first day without fast, formal follow up and expect to build a strong relationship with the person.

By following the prescribed activities and others like them, you will accomplish the following:

1. Make a much better impression on the new employee as a professional organization.
2. Give the direct supervisor the opportunity to establish a strong relationship with the new hire.
3. More quickly calm a new hire's apprehensions and anxiety, which will help him or her reach higher levels of productivity faster.
4. Improve your chances of retaining the employee for the long term.
5. Create greater clarity of what you expect and by when, which eliminates confusion and excuses for nonperformance.

Learn from Maslow

If you've ever studied Maslow's motivational hierarchy of needs then you know that, until a person is satisfied that he or she can survive and will be able to meet his or her basic life needs, no speeches about being part of a great team or having the potential to make unlimited income will stir an employee for very long. New employees begin to make decisions about whether or not this basic survival need is being met very early on in the job. If they are tossed to the wolves with no guidance or training; if they suspect that management doesn't really care about them but only about what they produce; or if they draw the conclusion that they're working in an unprofessional workplace that burdens them with poverty wages while promising a sky-is-the-limit income, by following their basic instinct to survive they will first mentally check out of the workplace and soon thereafter leave it physically.

Right Hook RULE

The longer and more effective you make your on-boarding program, the greater the chances of retaining the employee over the long-term. You really will reap what you sow.

Standing Eight-Count Questions

1. Are your performance and behavioral expectations in writing so that new hires understand what is expected of them in these regards?
2. How long is your on-boarding process for new employees?
3. Do you assign and pay a mentor to help new hires have a softer landing once joining your organization?
4. Do you have written job descriptions for each position in your organization?
5. Do you use a checklist of essential tasks that a supervisor completes at the end of a new employee's first day on the job?
6. What is the cost to you in terms of time and money when you must replace a front-line employee? A manager?
7. What is your strategy for highly structuring a new hire's first day?
8. Do you pay enough so that a new employee's need for survival, as per Maslow's hierarchy of needs, is met so he or she can focus on the work at hand?

Notes

ROUND 8

How to Retain Eagles Once You Find Them

Opening Bell

Do you remember the movie "Field of Dreams" with Kevin Costner? Costner played a man obsessed by a vision to turn his cornfield into a baseball diamond in order to attract star players from the past. A voice persisted in telling him, *"If you build it, they will come."* Well, he built it and they did indeed come. The same holds true for building an eagle environment. If you want to attract and retain the best possible people into your organization you must make your workplace one of your most compelling recruiting and retention tools. In the last business that I ran we instituted a "Top 20 Percent Club" that showered additional support, recognition, rewards, and opportunities on our top people and, lo and behold, word got around the market place and before long we had eagles in other organizations coming to us looking for a job.

Run a meritocracy not a welfare state.

The Top Performer's Club

Do you have any sort of top performer's club that sends a message to your employees that you are committed to supporting and rewarding excellence? If not, get creative and think about how you can do so. Following are a few guidelines that will get you started:

1. Run the competition for the club so that people qualify every 60 days or quarterly at the most.
2. Keep the criteria for winning entrance into the club simple.
3. If you have a smaller department and the concept of a "Top 20 percent" of your employees is not feasible, then refer to the club as a "Top Gun,""Presidents," or "Platinum Club" where everyone meeting certain criteria receives the perks, recognition, and support.
4. Offer a combination of tangible and recognition rewards along with additional support (like a temp to help with administrative work and so forth) so that you not only reward the performer but also help him or her reach an even higher level of performance.
5. Anyone remaining in the club for an entire year should receive a meaningful grand prize: a special trip or a significant cash reward and so forth.

Eagles and turkeys don't eat the same food.

Stop Hugging and Burping the Fellowship of the Miserable

Unfortunately, many business cultures are little more than glorified welfare states wherein the bottom performers get most of the time, attention, and favors as managers engage in fruitless efforts to elevate the miserable up to mediocre. This sends a dangerous message to your best people because it says in essence, "When you get really good and excel at your job, what you can expect in return from me is less time and attention."

In addition to the top performer's club as outlined previously, review the following traits and strategies for creating an eagle environment. Measure your own company against these criteria to see what kind of job you've done to build a culture that will attract and retain the best people while you weed out the sluggards, and to recognize where you still have work to do in both areas as well.

Left Jab Laws—Eagle Environment Traits

1. Managers spend more time with people-work than paperwork.
2. Top performers are rewarded with special perks, opportunities, recognition, and support.
3. Promotions are based on performance and not on tenure.
4. You implement pay raise policies that reward results and not requests.
5. Management has implemented minimum performance standards and poor performers are terminated if they are unable to meet them. In this manner, your top people are protected from the burden of having to share the workplace with sluggards or misfits.
6. Fairness is defined as giving people what they have earned and deserve based on past performance; not as treating everyone the same.

Right Hook RULE

"There is nothing more unequal than the equal treatment of unequals."

—Vince Lombardi

7. The managers give honest feedback. If an employee is great, they tell him or her. If someone is failing, they point that out as well.
8. Ample opportunities are given for an employee to learn and grow through training and mentoring.
9. Top performers are given more latitude and discretion so that they can make certain decisions and implement ideas without having to check with higher ups.

Right Hook RULE

The number one reason good people leave an organization is to pursue personal growth opportunities elsewhere.

Corporate Welfare State Traits

The next nine points are characteristics of a corporate welfare state, where the strong are weakened in order to strengthen the weak. Just as in the eagle evaluation, honestly assess your organization's culture against the following criteria and realize how difficult these conditions make it to define your business culture as a high-performance place where top performers come to reach their potential.

1. Pay raises are given out of ceremony and not because people earned them.
2. Christmas bonuses are given because it is Christmas time and not because people went the extra mile.
3. The first person considered for a promotion is the person with the most tenure, not necessarily the most capable person for the job.
4. Tenured people have become lazy and have retired on the job because they're no longer held accountable.

Right Hook RULE

Tenure can become a license for laziness. Your number one concern should be the high number of unemployed people you have on your payroll.

5. Managers sugarcoat, trivialize, and marginalize the truth rather than tell employees they're failing.
6. Managers would rather be well liked and popular than hold someone accountable.
7. Managers persist in doing what is easy, cheap, popular, or convenient rather than what is right...and oftentimes difficult.
8. Experience, tenure, or credentials substitute for results.
9. Managers tolerate poor performers for far too long.

Right Hook RULE

It is very bad business economics to weaken the strong in order to strengthen the weak.

Who Gets Preferential Treatment?

Sadly, in many organizations the top performers are actually treated worse than bottom performers. Before you go into denial, answer these three questions:

With whom do you spend most of your time: the top people or those at the bottom? In most cases a manager spends so much time at the bottom acting as a savior of lost causes while engaging in another rescue mission that he or she virtually ignores the top people.

If you run a sales organization, to whom do your managers most often give "house deals"? If you're like most companies, the house deals are dished out to the bottom dwellers just so they can make a paycheck rather than distributed to the people who have earned and deserve them based on their unequal contribution to the team's success.

What type of conversations do you have with each category of performer on your team? Again, in most cases, managers exhort the folks at the bottom with happy hot-tub talk phrases like: "I believe in you; I know that you can make it; I knew you could do it," and the like. On the other hand, the words normally tossed in the direction of their top performers sound something like this: "Don't get lazy on me; You let me down last month; I really need you to step it up this month."

If the three prior points resemble what goes on in your business then you'll have a very difficult time hiring eagles and an impossible job keeping them and helping them develop to their potential.

The Power of Leveraging Your Strengths

I know that what I'm about to say is unconventional so even though you may not agree with it at first, please keep an open mind and give it a fair hearing: The people in your organization who still have the highest upward potential are those already doing the best! That's right. What I'm saying is that it is your best performers who still have the most potential for growth in your organization. Why? Precisely because top performers do so well the managers stop paying attention to them, developing them, and supporting them and, thus, they eventually plateau and never come close to reaching their fullest potential. If most managers would exert just a fraction of the effort they expend on cellar-dwellers and re-appropriate that time into the growth of their best people, the results they'd reap would blow the roof of the place.

Unfortunately, some readers will start spending more time with their best performers and make things worse rather than better. This is because during the time they spend with their eagles they will micromanage, nit-pick, or otherwise get in the way. They will distract and demoralize the person rather than help bring him or her up to a higher performance level. If this is what you're going to do when you spend time with your best people then it is probably best if you do ignore them! Spending time with great people is most productive when you do so in a supportive way. In other words, you brainstorm with them on what it will take to get them to the next level and you ask them questions like: "What do you need from me in order to become more successful?," "What additional support or resources do you need?," and "What obstacles are standing in the way of the greater performance that I can get out of you?"

Right Hook RULE

It's easier to elevate a good performer to great status then it is to bring the miserable performers up to a level of mediocrity because the good performers give you something to work with: a foundation of talent, drive, attitude, character, energy, discipline, and skills.

The Manager as a Magnet

Keep this in mind as you create an eagle environment: You need great managers in place to attract, develop, and retain eagles. Incapable managers are one of the key reasons a solid performer leaves an organization. An eagle is simply not going to let his or her potential rot on the vine while a Bozo with a manager's name badge tries to get his or her own act together and inflicts a cruel form of amateur hour on highly capable and motivated people. To get help developing your managers or your own management and leadership ability, read and apply the ten knockout strategies in *TKO Management* (Wiley, 2007) immediately after completing this book.

One final thought: Don't expect to get a shot at attracting too many eagles in the first place if your compensation plans offer "unlimited potential" anchored by a guaranteed promise of poverty. Many sales organizations are famous for this. They run ads with "sky's the limit" income potential based on commissions with a guaranteed base salary of between $1,000 and $1,500 per month; which is precisely the rate of poverty-line wages in the United States for families of two and four, respectively. The bottom line is that if an eagle in an unrelated industry considers switching over to your field there will be two fears that stop him or her from making the leap: the poverty factor and the spouse factor. In other words, not too many salespeople will give up their current high five or low six figure income job to switch careers and work for a minimum of promises of poverty. Secondly, even if they decide to roll the dice, they'd never be able to convince their spouse to support the move. Could you just imagine the conversation: "Honey, I'm bored with selling computer systems and I'd like to try something new. I'm going into the automotive retail business. They're going to guarantee me $1,000 per month, 6-day work weeks, and long hours, but because of its unlimited potential there's a chance I will make more than the

$80,000 I took in last year working for IBM." Resign yourself that expecting a potential eagle to make such a move is the same as asking that he part with 50% of his assets and see his kids only on weekends.

Right Hook RULE

Share the risk in order to attract and hire an eagle. If an applicant can verify that he or she made $80,000 last year, guarantee him or her $6,500 per month for the first 90 days to give him or her a softer landing and take the fear out of discovering the "unlimited potential" in your enterprise.

Standing Eight-Count Questions

1. Which of the eagle environment traits listed are found in your workplace?
2. Which of the corporate welfare traits listed are found there?
3. Do you have a top performer's club?
4. With whom do you spend more of your time: top or bottom performers?
5. Which of your top performers must you commit to spending more time and effort with so that you can help them develop their potential?
6. Which of your bottom performers must you turn around quickly or remove so they don't continue to drain your resources?
7. When you currently spend time with your best people do you have encouraging and supportive conversations or do you primarily challenge them to do even better than they're doing without bringing closure to what they've already done well?
8. If you were an eagle looking for a job, would you go to work in your place of business?

Notes

ROUND 9

Differentiate Your Employees for Development and Retention

Opening Bell

While preparing to speak to a group of five hundred plus H.R. managers in Hong Kong I began to have second thoughts as to whether or not one of the primary thrusts of my message "give your best to the best and less to the rest" would resonate with my audience. After all, even though the economy was booming in China, it was still under communist rule where the "weaken the strong to strengthen the weak to create a level playing field for all" was at the bedrock of their political philosophy. During the luncheon after my speech, I was gratified and relieved to have multiple attendees tell me that the part of my message they liked best was the "give your best to the best and less to the rest" strategy I had presented. As one businessman explained, "In the years during and after Mao, doctors were paid the same as farmers in the name of keeping everything and everyone equal. That philosophy held us back from a more intelligent allocation of our resources and we've been playing economic catch-up ever since."

Right Hook RULE

Great leaders don't try to reward, spend time with, or develop everyone on their teams with the same cookie-cutter strategy. Instead, they differentiate their teams into three groups of people and create a separate strategy for each group.

Defining A, B, & C Players

Astute leaders differentiate the people on their teams. They have separate strategies for the three different groups of people they're responsible for, with the goal of drawing more productivity out of each group. These leaders also understand that, without the right players on the teams, the quality of your strategy is irrelevant since "C" players cannot successfully execute an "A" strategy. Thus, they are not afraid to differentiate their employees. They don't do so to pass judgment but to assess performance because the sole objective of differentiation is to improve performance.

Right Hook RULE

A great dream with the wrong team is a nightmare!

While the natural tendency is to differentiate players at the lower rungs of the ladder, top leaders begin molding their teams by differentiating managers. This is because there's much more at stake when it comes to developing managers since they will either elevate or devastate the people in their charge.

"A" Players Definition: They define standards for exceptional performance; inspire and motivate others by consistently delivering results.

"B" Players Definition: Solid performers who meet expectations but may have limited upward mobility.

"C" Players Definition: Barely deliver acceptable results and oftentimes bring results less than acceptable.

None of the three classifications is a permanent verdict on an employee. Stars can fall and strugglers can rise depending on internal and external motivation, skill development, a change in an immediate supervisor or in responsibilities, and more.

Characteristics Of and Strategies for "A" Players

Generally, this group will be made up of your top 20% of employees. This group is more demanding to lead. They are less likely to be impressed with you and may even feel that they know more than you or are more capable than you. They oftentimes require more of your attention and will stretch and challenge you. They constantly come up with new initiatives and ideas. But that's how they grow and if you don't spend time with these players they will leave the organization.

A. Accelerate their growth with jobs that stretch them. Give them more latitude and discretion. This not only retains them but also maximizes their ability to contribute to the business. It also makes them less dependent on you, which is a prime motivator for them.

B. Spend time with them personally as a priority and give them continual positive and constructive feedback so they can keep growing.

C. Pay them substantially more. Don't play ego games with your best people's pay. Too often I'll see an arrogant boss lose a top performer over money issues. Oftentimes the star takes other good people with him or her to the next place of employment. Once the business of the stingy leader's company starts to decline, he's on the phone offering the dearly departed more money to return. This is stupidity on steroids. If you'd pay more to get top performers back then go ahead and pay them now so they don't leave and break your momentum, lower morale, and diminish your credibility.

Right Hook RULE

The most expensive people on your payroll are not the highest paid. The most expensive people on your payroll are the unproductive people.

Characteristics Of and Strategies for "B" Players

This group will probably make up the majority of your employees. Thus, they are the backbone of your organization.

A. Affirm their strengths and be honest about their shortcomings so you can increase their performance.

B. Invest in their development through training and personally mentoring the best of this group. This energizes and helps retain them.

C. Give them intrinsic rewards including plenty of recognition, trust, and clear communication. Pay them well.

D. Recognize accomplishments with new opportunities. Some of these will become "A" players.

Right Hook RULE

If you fail to recognize and reward "A" players as a priority, you've given "B" players little to emulate or to look forward to.

Characteristics Of and Strategies for "C" Players

Normally, this group constitutes your bottom 10 to 20% of performers. They are often the result of hiring errors or of placing someone into a role for which he or she is not fit.

Right Hook RULE

If you're going to spend inordinate amounts of time and resources trying to convert strugglers to survivors, you'll have little left for the truly rewarding work of stretching your good players into great ones.

A. These people stay in a comfort zone, think incrementally, and maintain rather than grow.
B. They slow others down because others must spend more time with them, clean up their messes, or help them carry their loads. No one clamors to work with them and they take more from an organization than they give to it.
C. Establish minimum performance standards that create a benchmark for acceptable performance. These people will

either stretch to hit the standards or fire themselves when they fail to do so.

D. If you currently have "C" players on the verge of termination, you should be clear with them about where they stand. They should also understand where they must be performance wise and by when as well as the consequences for failing to attain. If you must later terminate them they should have seen it coming and not be caught by surprise.

Right Hook RULE

Make certain that if you have an HR department that they fully understand that their role is to accelerate the removal of poor performers and not to block their exodus.

Separate the Person from the Performance

These are not bad people so don't make it personal. Love the performer and hate the performance. In fact, care enough about the person to confront him or her when they are off track and help him or her right their course. Resist the temptation to try and become a management hero by thinking you're the one person on earth who can turn this person around and make him or her into a superstar. The fact is that regardless of how much potential you see in the person, without results your own reputation and effectiveness begin to suffer. It is perfectly acceptable to work with someone in accordance with their potential for a period of time but eventually you must work with him or her in accordance with their bottom-line performance.

Right Hook RULE

Continue to invest in people as long as they make measurable progress in reasonable time. But, once they begin to hover at or below average performance levels with no sign of improvement, it's time to help them move on and discover their future someplace else.

Many "C" players are often left behind because of deficient skills or because they are cast in the wrong roles. Often times, they were "B" players but the organization outgrew them. The cost of removing these people cannot be trivialized, but the cost of not doing so is much greater. This is especially true when you consider the fact that you probably tend to keep the wrong people too long. They just hang around making a mess of things. And to make matters worse, when "C" players are not addressed, it makes others in the organization feel the company is being poorly managed.

Right Hook RULE

The number one cause of turnover is hiring the wrong person in the first place.

Standing Eight-Count Questions

1. Who are your "A" players? (List on a separate sheet of paper.)
2. What is your current strategy to develop these people? Be specific.
3. Who are your "B" players? (List on a separate sheet of paper.)
4. What is your current strategy to develop these people? Be specific.
5. Who are your "C" players? (List on a separate sheet of paper.)
6. What is your strategy to turnaround or remove these people?
7. Which hiring strategy from this book will you implement that will help you to hire more "A" players?
8. Which hiring strategy can you employ to fire "C" players before you hire them.

Notes

ROUND 10

Knockout Summary for Follow-Through

Let's conclude with a knockout summary of key points from each Round. Each Round summary will include key points and an occasional question to help you evaluate your progress. Review these notes often as a catalyst to consistent action. This is the most important strategy of all because, if you fail to follow through—you fail.

Right Hook RULE

The biggest gap in business is the gap between knowing and doing. To elevate your organization, you must develop the discipline to close this gap.

Knockout Summary

Round One: Understand the Cost of Hiring Recklessly

1. People are not your greatest asset—the right people are!
2. Hiring recklessly diminishes results, breaks momentum, lowers morale, and destroys your personal credibility.

3. Poor performers hurt you the most when you have momentum.
4. Hire slow; fire fast.
5. Hiring should be an elimination process, not an inclusive process.
6. The best time to fire is before you hire.
7. What is your proactive, long-term recruiting strategy using the many examples offered in Round one? Which strategies have you already implemented and which will you address next?
8. What have you done to develop a rigorous interview process? This includes asking the right questions, looking for the right traits, setting the person up for counter offers, and creatively checking references. What behavioral-based questions can you add to those given?
9. Have you begun predictive testing to determine whether the candidate is bringing the internal un-teachables, necessary for excellence, to the workplace?
10. What have you done to create an eagle environment and weed out any aspects of a corporate welfare state?
11. Have you defined your "A," "B," and "C" players and what is your strategy for each group?

Right Hook RULE

Life rewards action! It doesn't reward experience, wisdom, or knowledge. Get up off your knowledge and do something!

Round Two: Become a Proactive Recruiter

1. The number one strategy for recruiting is getting proactive!
2. There is no shortage of talented people. It's just that the most talented, productive, and effective people already have jobs!

3. Use your web site as a recruitment post and allow people to apply online.
4. Market to your customer base.
5. Use "Eagle Calling Cards."
6. Create and be able to communicate a compelling EVP.
7. Turn everyone in your organization into a recruiter and pay them well and quickly when they refer a new employee.
8. Word your want-ads so they attract people looking for opportunities, not those looking for paychecks!
9. Managers should take more personal responsibility for finding great people for their teams. They must go from waiting to be hunted to being the hunter.
10. Use employment web sites to search resumes and post your own job openings.
11. Debrief new hires for additional referrals.
12. Raid talent pools when uncertainty reigns.
13. Use the radio as a medium to attract passive job candidates.

Round Three and Round Four: Create a Potent Interview Structure and Ask Tough Interview Questions

The summary for these two Rounds is combined because they tie so closely together and one builds logically upon the other.

1. An interview is a fact-finding expedition not a casual conversation or a sales pitch.
2. The number one cause of hiring errors is making emotional decisions during the interview based on personalities, appearance, biases, or stereotypes.
3. Define job descriptions and performance expectations for each position you hire and go over them with the candidate during the interview. If you want great job performance you must first define it.
4. Direct your interview to focus more on past accomplishments than past experience.

5. Prestructure your interview questions in advance and make sure they are behavioral based.
6. It is not necessary to ask a large number of questions. Instead, ask a handful of the right questions and then dig deep for specifics when you get an answer. The deeper you dig the more exaggeration you will weed out.
7. Don't judge people strictly by where they are in life. Also consider the obstacles they had to overcome to get there.
8. A short telephone interview will help reduce the impact of a visual first impression and make you more objective when you actually meet the person live.
9. Remember that there is a significant difference between interview performance and job performance. Focus on hiring those good at doing the job . . . not those who excel at getting the job!
10. Throughout the interview process, remain the buyer.
11. Before you make a firm financial offer, test the waters by suggesting a range and see how the candidate responds to it.
12. Throughout the interview process, listen at least four times as much as you speak.
13. Build your team around individual excellence—talented people—not just the easy-to-manage or harmonious job candidate.
14. Keep highly developed leaders involved in the interview process.
15. Have several key people interview the candidate.
16. Plant seeds to fend-off counter offers.
17. Remind the candidate of the competition.
18. When hiring, don't focus on the possible exception!
19. You can teach skills and knowledge but you can't teach talent, energy, drive, character, or attitude. You must hire these traits in.

20. During the interview, delve deeply into the candidates' past track record because the best predictor of future performance is past performance. This will also help determine whether or not they have the five un-teachable traits listed.
21. Ask some stressful questions to see if the candidates can handle high-pressure and awkward situations before they're on your payroll.

Round Five: Effectively Check References

1. Get creative when checking references.
2. Lower defenses and ask nonthreatening questions.
3. Check with the former subordinates of the person you're interviewing as they are less guarded in their replies.
4. Ask for one additional reference that the candidate has not listed.

Round Six: How to Use Predictive Testing Hiring Profiles

1. Understand the truth about "unlimited potential." Human beings don't have it at everything!
2. Use predictive testing to help determine if job candidates have the inside traits you cannot teach them.
3. Remember that excellence is impossible without talent.
4. Talent, while a great head start, is still only potential. This is why you must also dig into candidates' track record to see what they've done with the talent they possess.
5. Use the profiles as a coaching tool after you've hired the candidates to help them develop strengths and diminish or manage around weaknesses.

Round Seven: How to Get New Hires Off to a Great Start

1. Create a longer and more effective on-boarding process for new employees as this improves retention and helps them develop to their potential.

2. Before you become discouraged by the time and dollar cost of developing someone, weigh out the cost of failing to do so and having to replace him or her.
3. Until employees feel secure in their jobs and that they will be able to survive, they cannot be motivated by opportunities to grow, future financial promises, or belonging to a great team.
4. Highly structure an employee's first day.
5. Set forth training, values, and performance expectations and review them with the employees very early in their tenure.
6. Have a senior manager/partner/owner spend some time with new employees sharing the company's history and story.
7. If you are the new hire's supervisor, stay personally involved in the on-boarding and orientation process and don't delegate it to an underling.

Round Eight: How to Retain Eagles Once You Find Them

1. Build an eagle environment that will retain your best people.
2. Eliminate traits of a corporate welfare culture that drain your best people's morale.
3. Give your best to the best and less to the rest.
4. Don't weaken the strong in order to strengthen the weak.
5. Initiate a top performer's club.

Round Nine: Differentiate Your Employees for Development and Retention

1. To get the most out of each player on your team, divide them into three groups and devise and implement a separate strategy for each group.
2. "A" players are normally your top 20% of performers.

3. "B" players are generally the middle 20% of your employees.
4. "C" players are the bottom 10 to 20%.
5. Pay top performers substantially more.
6. Work according to employees' potential for a while, but eventually you must treat them in accordance with their results.

Notes

Bibliography

Adler, Lou. 1998. *Hire With Your Head*. Hoboken, NJ: Wiley.

Anderson, Dave. 2003. *Up Your Business*. Hoboken, NJ: Wiley.

Greenberg, Herbert, Harold Weinstein, & Patrick Sweeney. 2001. *How to Hire and Develop Your Next Top Performer*. New York: McGraw Hill.

Index

Made in the USA
Columbia, SC
10 January 2021